Duets for Strings

BY

SAMUEL APPLEBAUM

FOREWORD

The Duets For Strings may be started when the pupil has reached Page 15 of Volume I of the String Builder. They may, however, be used in conjunction with any standard string class Method, and may be used after the student has learned to use the first three fingers on the D and A strings. These Duets may be played by:

two Violins	Violin and Viola	Viola and Cello	Cello and Bass
two Violas	Violin and Cello	Viola and Bass	
two Cellos	Violin and Bass		
two Basses			

Starting on Page 2, we have the 2 3 finger pattern, which means that the 2nd and 3rd fingers are a half-step apart and are placed close to each other. Starting from Page 6, F natural and C natural are introduced, which gives us the 1 2 finger pattern, with the first and second fingers a half-step apart. Starting on Page 8, we play F natural on the E string, which is the 0 1 finger pattern. This means that there is a half-step between the open E string and the first finger, F. As always, the remaining fingers are a whole step apart.

The two slanted lines (//) mean that the bow is to be lifted from the string. This is done usually at the end of a phrase. Its purpose is to make the pupil cognizant of the architecture of each duet by pointing out the phrases. Lifting and re-setting the bow helps to develop control of the bow arm.

The comma (❜) means a slight pause, also usually at the end of a phrase, with the bow remaining on the string. This usually occurs when the phrase ends on the down bow above the middle of the bow.

To conform with the String Builder, the accidentals are placed before each note rather than in the signature.

E. L. 1990

2

1. For the first eight duets we use the $\hat{2}\,3$ finger pattern which means that the 2nd and 3rd fingers are a half step apart and placed close to each other.
2. Keep the finger on the string throughout the length of the line next to the fingering.
3. Leave a slight pause at each comma, with the bow remaining on the string. Lift the bow at the slanted lines (//).

1. Pastoral

L. Köhler

2. The Journey

Th. Henning

E. L. 1990

1. In duet Number 3, count carefully on the half rests.
2. In duet Number 4, lift the bow at each quarter rest starting down bow on the next note.

3. The Birch Canoe

Th. Henning

(MELODY)

4. The Nutcracker

L. Schubert

(MELODY)

E. L. 1990

4

1. Notice that in these duets there are three beats to each measure.
2. In duet Number 6, count the whole rests very carefully.

5. Counting Song

L. Köhler

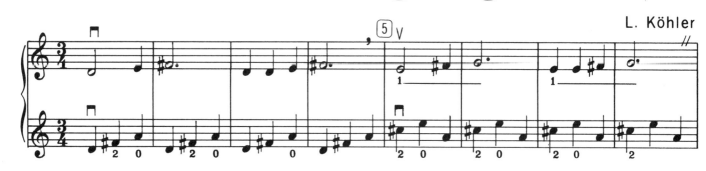

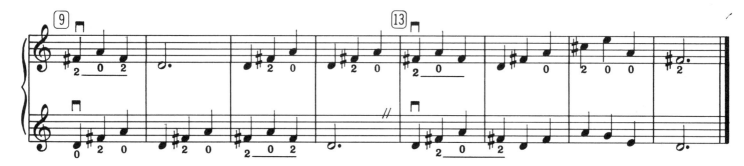

6. Waltz of the Flowers

Old Dance Song

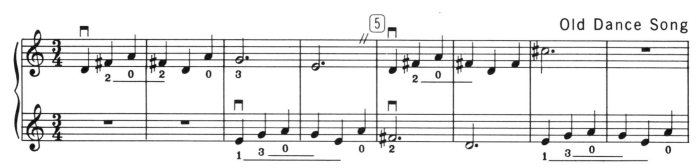

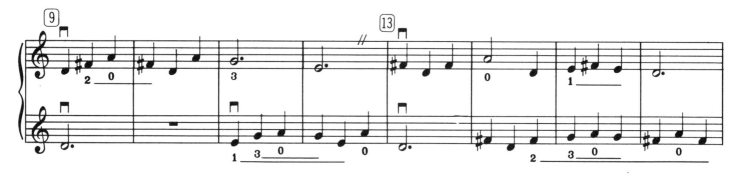

E.L.1990

When you play two notes in the same bow stroke, divide the bow evenly.

7. Two to a Bow

F. Beyer

8. The Island Song

F. Wohlfahrt

6

1. In these duets, we play F♮ and C♮ on the D and A strings. This gives us the 1̂ 2 finger pattern with the 1st and 2nd fingers a half step apart.

2. Notice that we now include the G string with the 2̂ 3 finger pattern. The 2nd and 3rd fingers, B and C are a half step apart.

9. Russian National Hymn

A. von Lvoff

10. The Swan

L. Schubert

E.L.1990

We start the fingers on the E string with the 1 2 finger pattern. The 1st finger F♯ is a whole step from the open string and the 2nd finger G, a half step from the 1st finger.

11. The Grand Canyon Waltz

F. Wohlfahrt

12. The Hunt

Old English

E. L. 1990

1. In Number 13, we play three notes in a bow. Use one third of the bow for each quarter note.
2. In Number 14, we play F♮ on the E string. This gives us the ⌢0 1 finger pattern with a half step between the open string and the 1st finger F. The remaining fingers are a whole step apart. Do not move the left thumb or wrist when playing the 1st finger close to the nut.
3. The notes marked with crosses (+) are to be plucked with the 4th finger of the left hand.

13. The Evening Waltz

F. Wohlfahrt

14. Picking with the Fourth

Old Dance Song

In Number 15, draw the bow a bit faster on the down-bow.

15. Gliding

Old Song

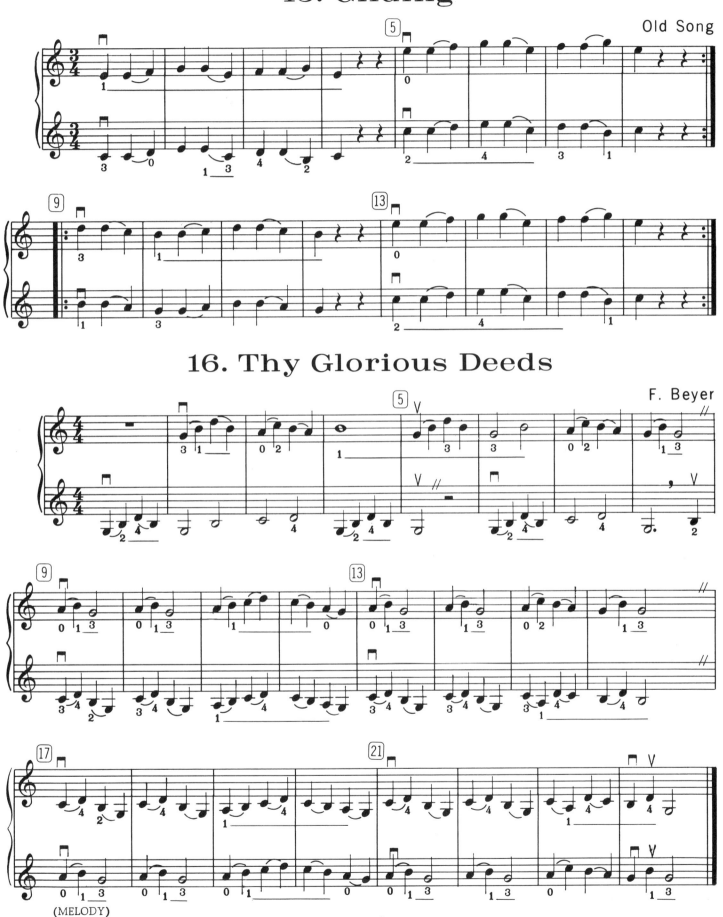

16. Thy Glorious Deeds

F. Beyer

(MELODY)

Here we continue to slur three notes in a bow. Use as much of the bow as you can, making sure that the bow does not slide down towards the fingerboard above the middle.

17. The Home Road

Anonymous

18. In the Garden

C. Hohmann

1. Play broadly on the notes marked "forte" (f). Use less bow on the passages marked "piano" (p). Be sure to maintain firm finger pressure of the left hand at all times.

2. In the last three measures, try to play both notes at the same time. If this is not possible, play only the top notes.

19. Sonatina

C. Dancla

1. Please observe the dynamic marks.
2. Where there are double notes (we call them double stops) you may play both together, or just the top notes.

20. Concertino

C. Dancla

1. Notice the eighth notes. Two eighth notes receive one count.
2. Grip the bow firmly for the eighth notes. Press the fingers of the left hand firmly in the strings so that the eighth notes will be distinctly heard.

21. Rejoice

F. Wohlfahrt

22. Elves Dance

F. Wohlfahrt

1. We now slur two eighth notes in the same bow.   Play them evenly.
2. In measures 7, 9 and 13 of Number 23, we have the 2nd finger on A which is placed close to the 1st finger, and the 2nd finger on D which is raised and placed close to the 3rd finger.   Listen carefully to these notes.

23. Listen to the Lambs

L. Köhler

24. Spring Plowing

F. Beyer

We hope that you have enjoyed playing these duets. Review most of the duets in this book playing each one twice. Change parts the second time.

25. Bagatelle

26. Do Re Mi Fa Sol

L. Köhler

E.L.1990

Music From Four Centuries
For String Orchestra

MUSIC FROM FOUR CENTURIES
(For String Orchestra)
transcribed by Samuel Applebaum

This series presents a variety of materials from six different composers spanning the 17th through 20th centuries. The arrangements are in the grade 2 to 3 level and each has a "mini" lesson plan printed at the top of the page. The book also gives the instructor materials to use to teach different styles and periods of music. **MUSIC FROM FOUR CENTURIES** is a good and economical way for an orchestra director to buy seven performance works in a good variety of style and content.

Includes:

- **MENUET** - G. F. Handel (1685-1759)
- **MOODS** - B. Bartók (1881-1945)
- **SARABANDE** - K. Böhm (1844-1920)
- **SERENADE FOR STRINGS** - W.A. Mozart (1756-1791)
- **SONATINA FOR STRINGS** - M. Clementi (1752-1832)
- **TO A WILD ROSE** - E. MacDowell (1861-1908)
- **TWO HUNGARIAN FOLK TUNES** - B. Bartók (1881-1945)

MUSIC FROM FOUR CENTURIES
(For String Orchestra)
transcribed by Samuel Applebaum

____ **Conductor** (EL 03710)
____ **1st Violin** (EL 03711)
____ **2nd Violin** (EL 03712)
____ **3rd Violin (Viola T. C.)** (EL 03713)
____ **Viola** (EL 03714)
____ **Cello** (EL 03715)
____ **String Bass** (EL 03716)
____ **Piano** (EL 03717)

This music is available at leading music dealers in the United States and Canada.